THE
Archive Photographs
SERIES
BILLINGSHURST

THE BILLINGSHURST NEWS.

No. 12.
New Series.

SATURDAY, NOVEMBER 2nd, 1935.

Issued Fortnightly.
Gratis.

R. RHODES & SON,

SOUTH STREET, BILLINGSHURST.

BOOT AND SHOE REPAIRS

OF ALL DESCRIPTIONS.

MODERN MACHINERY.

Rubber Wellingtons Repaired Efficiently.

BOOT & SHOE SUNDRIES.

R. CRISP,

HIGH STREET, BILLINGSHURST.

High-Class Tobacconist.

LADIES' AND GENT.'S HAIRDRESSER.

All Brands of Tobacco and Cigarettes.

Films Developed and Printed.

Established 29 years.   Phone 37.

JUBILEE MEMORIAL TREES.

The roadside bank in South Street has been planted with a row of 14 flowering cherry trees as a memorial to the Silver Jubilee of H.M. the King and Queen. They are of two shades of pink, *Hisakura* and *J. B. Veitch.* The trees were supplied by Mr. and Mrs. R. E. Norris and the Misses Puttock, who each planted a tree, The planting was completed by Mr. G. Radbourne, senr., and Mr. P. Wood, jnr.

BILLINGSHURST BONFIRE SOCIETY.

The celebrations will take place on Wednesday, November 6th, and the Society are endeavouring to make them worthy of this Jubilee Year. A Spectacular Firework Display has been arranged with Messrs. Brocks, and the Fancy Dress Torchlight Procession will be much larger than for some years. Three bands have kindly offered their services : Billingshurst, Rudgwick, and West Chiltington. The Storrington Fire Brigade and the Horsham St. John Ambulance will also take part. The procession will start from the King's Head at 7 p.m., and will take its usual course, the Bonfire and Fireworks being lighted in Mr. Skinners field at the top of Osier Hill.

Judging for the Fancy Dress Competition will take place in the Village Hall before the Procession, at the following times : Juveniles 5.45 p.m. Ladies 6.0. Gentlemen 6.15. The Hall will be thrown open to the Public after the judging.

Many fine prizes are offered in the Fancy Dress Competition, particulars of which can be had from Mr. M. Butler, (opposite the Post Office).

FOOTBALL.

BILLINGSHURST F.C.

The Saturday Club has not yet been successful, although the last two games were more even than the scores show. The home match with Broadbridge Heath on October 19th was lost by 5 goals to 3, J. Matthews and W. Mabey (2) scoring for Billingshurst. At Horsham on October 26th the Terriers beat Billingshurst by 5 goals to 2, the latter scorers being R. Denman and J. Craven.

It would appear that the defence requires strengthening, as they have had 28 goals scored against them so far in the five League matches, while the forwards have scored 10.

EDITORIAL.

The " Billingshurst News " is published fortnightly and is gratis. Readers residing out of the Distribution area may obtain copies from tradesmen advertising in the paper. Include it in your order for goods. Copies will be posted direct for an annual subscription of 5/-, payable in advance. All communications should be addressed : " Billingshurst News," Tiller's Printing Works, Billingshurst.

The Billingshurst News was a free newspaper, the first edition was launched in 1929 and it was issued fortnightly for ten years. The paper was financed by the advertisements and it was very unusual for a village to have such a publication at this time. The shortage of paper at the beginning of the Second World War forced its closure. Charles Tiller was the editor and main journalist, he also printed the paper in a shed on the brow of Alicks Hill.

THE
Archive Photographs
SERIES

BILLINGSHURST

Compiled by
Wendy Lines

CHALFORD

First published 1995
Copyright © Wendy Lines, 1995

The Chalford Publishing Company
St Mary's Mill, Chalford,
Stroud, Gloucestershire, GL6 8NX

ISBN 0 7524 0301 X

Typesetting and origination by
The Chalford Publishing Company
Printed in Great Britain by
Redwood Books, Trowbridge

Cover photograph
Mr Shelley and his staff outside the "Inter", in the 1930s.

For my husband, Peter,
who is Billingshurst born and bred.

Contents

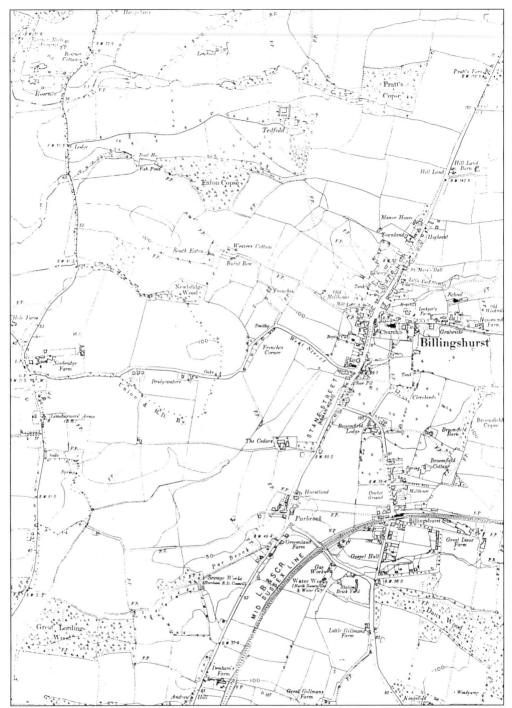

O S Map of the station area, Parbrook, the village and the western side of the parish, 1913. The parish extends from Adversane in the south to Five Oaks in the north; the course of the river Arun has been the western boundary since 1933; the eastern boundary extends beyond West Chiltington Lane.

An aerial view of the village c. 1934, which shows the Roman road of Stane Street disappearing into the distance towards Five Oaks. The street, which bisects the parish is one of the main reasons for the growth of the site of the village.

Introduction

Some charming early paintings and drawings exist of the Parish Church and High Street, as several artists have lived in the parish, in both this century and the last. There are also fascinating Victorian photographs, but most of the views of the village are from the humble picture postcard. Inexpensive enough for all to buy, the hey-day of the postcard was the Edwardian era. The postal service was very efficient and cards were often sent for rapid communication, rather like we use the telephone today.

Billingshurst never had an early resident photographer, although over the years several tradesmen commissioned postcards and a number of firms printed cards of Billingshurst. The views that are left give an enchanting picture of a bygone community, but there are a few places, both in the village and the parish of which no early photograph has so far come to light. Many of the early cards were carefully posed, some artistically with children, while others show the roads devoid of traffic very unlike the present.

All four Victorian drawings in the book are by members of the Evershed family. The earliest drawing dates from the 1840s, by that time Billingshurst was a self-contained, but not isolated agricultural parish of 1,439 inhabitants.

William Cobbett said in his *Rural Rides*, "Soon after quitting Billingshurst I crossed the river Arun, which has a canal running along- side of it. At this there are large timber and coal yards and kilns for lime. This appears to be a grand receiving and distributing place." He had previously had breakfast at the King's Arms and was served cream by the landlady's son, who was dressed in a faded smock mended with brightly coloured patches. "The sight of this smock-frock brought to my recollection many things dear to me. The boy, will, I dare say, perform his part at Billingshurst or some place not far from it."

This and other nineteenth century reminiscences made the village seem idyllic, but life in the 1840s was hard. Several inhabitants were transported for non-violent offences. There were man traps in Rowfold Orchard until 1867, and there is even an incidence of wife selling noted in Henry Burstow's *Tales of Old Horsham*, involving people from the village.

In the latter half of the nineteenth century conditions began to improve, both economically and socially, the latter owing not only to state intervention, but also on a smaller scale to the generosity of some of the wealthier local residents.

Towards the end of the nineteenth century leisure interests broadened. People travelled on railway excursions and cycling became very popular and photography became more widespread. More changes took place after 1918. Tom Topper, who was born and bred in the village and is now in his eighties said, "After the First World War charabancs used to come through the village. As they came over the hill, we used to call 'Throw out your coppers.' The coaches were going to Goodwood Races. When I was a boy Goodwood was a big week and there were lots of traffic and we would collect several pennies, but the police stopped it because it was dangerous. I mean kids were running all over the road picking up pennies amongst the traffic although it was only going at twenty-five miles an hour."

Vehicles did not travel at this slow speed for long. Progress generally and higher wages heralded the age of the motor car and the village would never be the same again, but it might be quieter once more if the long awaited by-pass is ever built!

It was not until after the Second World War that Billingshurst expanded rapidly. By 1991 the population had grown to over 5,000. Although some inhabitants are still occupied in agriculture, many more commute or are employed in the industrial estates, thus for the first time in its history Billingshurst has grown to small town size.

One

Viewing the Village

Rent was paid to the church for five shops as early as the sixteenth century. Some of the old buildings in the village have been shops for centuries, while other early timber-framed properties were farmhouses or inns. In the village area there are over twenty timber-framed houses which date mainly from the sixteenth century. Some important old buildings have been lost comparatively recently, but many more remain, the timbers of some are hidden beneath later brick façades. The old buildings were constructed from sturdy English oak, of which there was a ready supply from the Wealden forest. Although there are examples of houses from all subsequent periods it is the picturesque timber-framed houses that are typical of the locality. Throughout the parish there are over sixty more timber-framed buildings, which would have originally been the homes of yeoman farmers. In later centuries these dwellings were often divided into cottages and farm labourers and villagers lived in them. At the time when many of the photographs were taken these old cottages were not highly rated by ordinary inhabitants, because many had not been modernised. It is only in recent years that some of the buildings have reverted to being one house again and the timber-framed dwellings have become desirable residences and attractive family homes.

Alick's Hill, looking north. This view was photographed in 1897, and ten years later was used "touched up" as an Edwardian post-card. In the original version the pony and trap were out of focus. On the right was a covered saw-pit used by the wheelwrights, which was situated opposite. The poplar trees, in the distance, were for many years local landmarks.

Alick's Hill in Edwardian times. The low building on the left was part of a wheelwright's premises. This and the other wheelwright's sheds were demolished in 1979. The large building in the background was the Congregational Church, now the United Reformed Church. The wares from the sixpenny bazaar cart would have been sold around the district.

The beginning of South Street in the 1930s. Cooter's Bakery used to be situated in the house that lies back, not the one with the advertisement. Cooter's bread was baked in an oven heated by faggots.

Cecil Rhodes outside his shop in the late 1930s, when the window display was entered in a competition advertising Philip's soles and heels. Rhodes is one of the oldest established family shops in the village.

The opening of the Women's Hall in November 1923. Edith and Ellen Beck had the hall built for the women of the parish and they were also benefactresses to all sections of the community, regardless of creed. The formidable looking, but generous Misses Beck are on either side of the front row. Between them are Dorothy Cripps and the Hon. Mrs Bruce, wife of the Prime Minister of Australia, who officially opened the hall. Middle row, left to right: Mrs Sherlock, Mrs Wadey and Mrs Tribe. Top row: Mrs Crisp, Miss Webb, Mrs Cripps, and an unknown man.

The Women's Hall in 1925. The Beck sisters were friends of Mrs Pankhurst and were pioneers in the progressive women's suffrage movement. The Women's Institute has met at the hall from 1923, but its facilities have been long since been used by all sections of local society.

The Mothers' Garden, also donated by the Misses Beck, which is next to the Women's Hall. Behind the original playground equipment the caretaker's cottage can be seen, this was first intended to be a garden pavilion, but by 1927 it had become the home of a resident caretaker.

An appealing view of South Street in 1907. South Street became part of the High Street in the 1950s. The white fencing surrounding a public well is just visible.

South Street c. 1918. The house on the extreme right was The Crescent School, one of several small private schools in Billingshurst in the earlier part of this century.

14

The Annual Hospital or a Club Day Parade, both of which have disappeared from village life with the coming of the welfare state. Club Days were organised by the Friendly Societies and were festive occasions in the village. The Hospital Parade was a larger affair, attended by the Friendly Societies and other organisations, with several bands in attendance.

E W Cripps, butchers shop, 1970. There has been a butcher's shop in this vicinity for over a hundred years. Cripps is the only old butcher's name retained in the village, although the family sold the business in 1972. The abattoir ceased to operate at that time and the shop moved next door.

The King's Arms in Edwardian times when John Butterworth Sisman was the landlord. The King's Arms has the distinction of being mentioned in several minor literary publications and one major one, *Rural Rides* by William Cobbett published in 1830. By the time Cobbett visited the village the turnpike system had made improvements to the notoriously bad condition of Sussex roads, and stage-coaches stopped at village inns.

The King's Arms, 1925, from a drawing by Frank Pattison. (See page 106) The King's Arms was mentioned as an inn as early as the seventeenth century. A small corn market was held in the Club Room of the King's Arms in the latter part of the last century.

Ye Olde Six Bells c. 1950, formerly called Taintlands. It has a continuous jetty or overhang and it is good example of a timber-framed building. The carpenter or builder, who orginally constructed the dwelling centuries ago, would have made up the frame of the house in his yard and would have later re-erected it on its chosen site. The gaps between the timbers were filled with wattle and daub. In this area houses were often roofed with heavy Horsham stone.

Interior of Ye Olde Six Bells in the 1920s, when gas lighting was still in use. In the last century the Six Bells was a beerhouse and only became a public house early in this century. It is reputed that there is a tunnel from the Six Bells to the church, which was used by smugglers!

The Inglenook Fireplace and Fireback of Ye Olde Six Bells. The fireback was made from the re-used pattern of an iron graveslab memorial commemorating Anne Forster. It is said that the fireback "Must not be moved or a curse will fall on the mover."

Ten Steps in 1907. The one storey shop to the left of the steps was built in 1895 and was the first premises of Crisp the hairdresser. The low building on the right was the Parish Room and both that and the adjoining house have been demolished.

The Floral Parade passing Ten Steps in 1910. The local press said that Billingshurst was "waking up" by holding the parade.

Laker's Refreshment Rooms with Accommodation for Cyclists *c.* 1920. and the "Bank Buildings and Stores" next door.

South Street in 1909, when a barn still stood on the site of the "Bank Buildings and Stores", now 68 and 70 High Street.

Causeway Cottage and part of Tithe Cottage, in 1959. At this time the houses were in a semi-derelict state, after being unoccupied for five years. Fortunately Mr and Mrs Barton had them restored and they survive to enhance the village green. The cottages, although now much altered, were once one Wealden hall house dating from the late fourteenth or early fifteenth century.

Joseph Luxford and his family outside their shop in 1892. Mrs Luxford managed the shop because Joe Luxford was a leading figure in village affairs. Besides being one of the original members of the Parish Council formed in 1895, he was a Churchwarden, secretary to the Working Men's Club, and secretary to the Flower Show Committee, outing organiser, and amateur dramatic performer. He owned the allotments in Little East Street where he also had a tennis court. He both played tennis and organised tournaments. He was a carrier and took goods to and from Horsham every day, except Wednesdays. Carriers played an important role in rural areas bringing goods otherwise unattainable to the village.

The Causeway *c.* 1880. Mrs Marten 1864-1960 said in her recollections "Where the Post Office and other new buildings now stand there was a meadow with a low brick wall upon which men used to sit and chat together about the affairs of the village." There are even some sheep grazing in the meadow in the centre of the village.

The Causeway *c.* 1906. The familiar dormer windows and shopfront have been added by the Luxford family to their home and shop, now 59 High Street.

Mill Lane in 1907. Where the children, dressed in "pinnys", pose is now the site of the busy Library Car Park.

The Old Mill House, which was situated near the site of the windmill. The house was demolished after the Second World War. William and Sarah Phillips are at the door. He was a railway porter at Billingshurst Station for thirty-three years.

The Causeway and Church from Mill Lane by Arthur Evershed, 1854. Arthur, later Doctor Evershed, was eighteen years old when he drew this view.

Mill Way *c.* 1920. The nearby mill burnt down on the night of 5th November, 1852. It is unknown whether the fire was connected with Bonfire Night!

The Post Office, built in 1902. In the early days of the telephone, the exchange was housed in the top storey. The post office part of the business moved to other premises in 1989 and the old building is used as a delivery office.

Arthur Gravett c. 1900, when he was employed as a telegraph boy. At this time Job Saunders Clark was postmaster. Letters arriving from London and Brighton were delivered at 7 and 11 am., and despatched at 12.30 and 8 pm.

High Street *c*. 1885, with two men chatting near what is today Books and Things.

High Street *c*. 1906. The ivy-clad house was Brick House, which has a long association with the doctors of the parish. Dr W H Hubert had his practice here for over forty years, until 1911. His son Dr W A Hubert moved to Rose Hill and the veterinary surgeon J Craft moved into Brick House. The building on the left with the posters was built as a grain store *c*. 1895.

An unidentified military funeral *c.* 1928. The Horsham firm of Rice Brothers opened a branch of their garage in the village by 1926. The oval roofed building was erected and the grain store incorporated into their premises.

High Street in 1933, when Rice Brothers had brick-built premises and the new Westminster Bank had replaced the more attractive Brick House.

Rice Bros *c.* 1950, when at least ten staff were employed. The business was taken over by Southern Counties Garages in 1970 and the premises have since been demolished to make way for the supermarket building.

Mr Shelley and his staff outside the "Inter", in the 1930s. The shop is now a chemist, but had a long history as a grocery and hardware store. In the last century it was also the post office. Peter Kensett owned the shop in the 1840s.

The High Street, *c*. 1906. Clark & Co was an old established grocery business, trading in Billingshurst for over fifty years, first at this shop and later at Bank Stores. The large detatched ivy-covered Carlton House was the Victorian home of one branch of the wealthy Puttock family.

Arthur Gravett, *c*. 1893, when he was a delivery boy for Clark & Co.

The High Street, *c.* 1910, when Carlton House had been divided into three shops. The first double shop was Field's Ironmonger's Store. Two established businesses moved into the other shops, R Crisp the hairdresser and W Tribe the butcher.

High Street in 1927. The Ironmonger's store, then Pilcher's, was for sale. The shop was bought by Robert Higgins, who eventually took over the other two shops. Today it is Austen & Co. Since the premises became a shop in 1909 it has always been a similar type of store.

The Billingshurst and District Central Meat Market Christmas display in 1908, complete with a cat on the upstairs windowsill! The shop was the first premises of W Tribe, the butcher and is now the Tandoori Village Restaurant, 42 High Street.

Alfred Jones, the watchmaker and jeweller c. 1929. The white tiles from when the shop was a butchers are still intact. A Jones also used to walk to the larger houses in the district to wind clocks and set them to the correct time.

The King's Head when J Stewart was Landlord, *c.* 1911. The building dates from the late eighteenth century and has always been an inn. In the early nineteenth century it was a staging post for the Comet coach.

"King's Head" Inn, Billingshurst.

- JOHN STEWART, -

Wine, Spirit & Cigar Merchant.

GARAGE.

Good Accommodation for Motorists, Cyclists, and Commercial Travellers.

ACCOMMODATION you will find
For travellers of every kind,
Most of those who come from far
Appreciate a good *Cigar*.
Whilst *Wine* and *Spirits* are to hand
And served at anyone's command.
Bright sitting-room and well-aired bed
You'll always get at the *"King's Head!"*

An advertisement from Mrs Buskin's *Coronation Advertising Souvenir*, 1911. Elizabeth Buskin published a detailed account of the Coronation Celebrations in the village. She concluded her booklet with seven pages of advertisements each with a description, in verse, of the business concerned.

The medieval Gingers House, the Georgian malthouse and its associated buildings *c.* 1930, which were situated adjacent to the King's Head. By the late 1920s the buildings and backyard had been converted into an hotel and tea gardens owned by Major and Mrs Abercrombie and called The Maltings.

The Maltings Hotel *c.* 1930. The barley hoist was used when the building was a brewery. There were at least three malthouses in the parish and so much barley was converted into beer in the Billingshurst area that in the middle of the nineteenth century a resident Excise Officer, William Coulson was appointed.

Part of the premises when it was used by The Malaya Garage *c*. 1950. By this time the distinctive conical oast tower had been dismantled. The remaining buildings were demolished *c*. 1966 to make way for the modern precinct, Jengers Mead.

A massive tie-beam and part of a crown-post in a bedroom, which was in the medieval house part of The Maltings. It was one of the finest timber-framed houses in the village giving its name, The Gingers, to that area of the village.

34

A garden view of The Maltings. Frances Garnet, Vicountess Wolseley, who was an authority on old Sussex houses, was invited by the owners to come and look at The Maltings in 1932. Lady Wolseley left an intesting account of the structure of the building but said that she would not have liked to stay there because 'The food was not A1'.

Waitresses in the garden of The Maltings in 1932.

The north end of the High Street *c*. 1930. Jengers, the house, with the Yuccas in the garden has also been demolished. Under the brick facade it was timber-framed like the houses opposite, which are fortunately still standing.

The Rising Sun Public House, *c*. 1907. This pub, which was situated opposite the old Village Hall, was bought by the Horsham brewer, Henry Mitchell, in 1859 for £260. It later became a private house, and has since been demolished. The prominent lamp standard was still lit by oil; street lighting was introduced into the village in 1895. Mr Bristow had to light the sixteen oil lamps, moonlight nights excepted, for ten shillings a week.

The Laker family outside their house, Whitehall c. 1900, which was situated at the north end of the village near the present Roman Way. Henry Laker senior bought the property in 1847 and used part of it as a shop. Henry made and sold saddles, boots and other leather goods He also owned the nearby Rope-walk where plough reins and wagon ropes were made.

The three Laker boys c. 1912. Left to right Alfred Henry, Herbert Thomas and John William, sons of Henry junior.

By the 1920s Alfred Laker had taken over the shop and installed the first petrol pump in the village. The business was sold after the Second World War and became a garage. The house was demolished and Whitehall Garage expanded, a garage still operates from the site, but the old name has been lost.

The Manor House, formerly the Manor of Bassett's Fee, Billingshurst's main home manor. However, in an earlier age many different manors held land in Billingshurst, therefore the parish was never dominated by one manor or powerful lord. The Manor is timber-framed under the brick facade, which was put on in Georgian times, later the bay windows were added. These have since been removed, improving the appearance of the house.

The High Street after The Old Village Hall was built in 1906. Called St Mary's Hall until 1921, the vicar the Revd J Stanley, gave the hall to the parish. It was not until 1991 that this Village Hall was replaced by a new one situated in Roman Way. The old hall has been converted into flats, thus preserving a good example of an Edwardian building.

Gravett's shop, now Oak Cottage, in 1907, with two smartly dressed young members of the family standing outside. Gravett's was a confectioners and baker's shop. There were three other bakers' shops in the village at this time and a loaf then cost $2\frac{3}{4}$d.

John Argent's shop, *c*. 1900, when it had a Horsham stone roof. The façade, once again, hid a superior timber-framed Wealden Hall house, now the site of Lloyds Bank 37 High Street. The well remembered Bernard Baker later owned the premises.

A crown-post from the roof of Bernard Baker's shop when it was being demolished in 1968. Dan Daniel took this photograph and spotted the antiquity of roof structure, but the building was too far dismantled to save. The crown-post was donated by Lloyds Bank to the then newly formed Weald and Downland Open Air Museum.

Bernard Baker's shop in 1937, after he had the front modernised. The store was decorated to celebrate the Coronation of King George VI.

TAKE A HOLIDAY

AT

BERNARD BAKER'S

EXPENSE.

You can save enough on your Holiday Clothes by dealing at B.B.'s.

IT'S COMING !

DEAD LEAVES! BONFIRE NIGHT! 'FLU! AND DOCTORS' BILLS!

See **BERNARD BAKER** about that **OVERCOAT**, **WARM UNDERWEAR**, and a Good, Substantial **Pair of Boots.**

REMEMBER! *Every Manufacturer we deal of is a Maker of repute.*

A summer and winter advertisemnt from *The Billingshurst News* in the 1930s. Bernard Baker was renowned for his humerous advertisements. On his retirement in 1959, a local reporter called him "The old master of the art of advertising."

Lusted's shop front decorated for the Coronation of King George VI, 1937, with a display promoting Bird's Custard Powder. The shop, which is now 41a High Street, was run by the Lusted family from 1930 to the late 1950s.

Les Lusted in his delivery van. There are only two digits in the telephone number which is very different from today.

Voice's Monumental Works, *c.* 1880. A number of different branches of the Voice family have lived in Billingshurst for centuries. Until recent years the building firm of Raymond Voice was situated in little East Street; this Voice family were descendants of the Voices who owned the Monumental works.

The same premises in the 1960s. The yard had disappeared and a one storey building and part of the house had become the third premises of Crisp the hairdresser. The other half of the building continues to be used as a florist and Mrs Rita Howard can be seen standing by the door.

Looking up East Street in 1907. The property on the corner was owned by descendants of Joe Luxford, until it became Burdocks in recent years. Before that, at various times, it was a grocer's shop known as Balls, Butlers and Barnes.

Churchgate c. 1911. In the nineteenth century a shop-wing was added to Churchgate, which is a seventeenth century timber-framed house. For many years it was a grocer's shop. When Billy Shepherd was the proprietor, he was reputed to be the the fattest grocer in Sussex. In the 1920s the property became a guest-house and now the shop-wing has been converted into a flat.

A garden view of The Vicarage, *c.* 1920. The vicarage was built in 1858 and designed by the well known Victorian architect S S Teulon.

St Mary's Church and the earlier vicarage in 1854 by Dr Arthur Evershed. The dormer windows in the nave roof were removed during the 1866 restoration of the church. The older vicarage was built in 1714.

The present Gratwicke Close was constructed on the site of Gratwicke House, which was built *c*. 1830. Edward Thomas Norris bought the house and surrounding land in 1898; in the same year Sir Edwin Lutyens, who was a friend of E T Norris, designed a billiard room to add to the aready imposing residence.

E T Norris on Prince Richard at the entrance to the coach-house and stable of Gratwicke in 1908. Local events were often held at Gratwicke during the residence of Mr Norris. The well documented 1911 Coronation Celebrations were held here. Mr Norris died the same year and his family sold the estate in 1923.

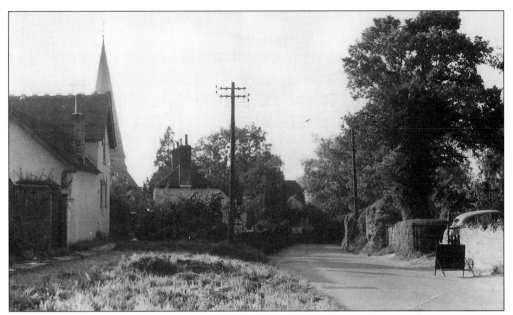

East Steet, c. 1958, Gratwick Lodge is on the left. This and the stable block are all that remains of Gratwicke House, which was requisitioned during the Second World War, and later became a guest-house. The house fell into disrepair and was demolished in the early 1960s.

Gordon Lugg's steam traction engines turning into his works in East Street, c. 1950. The back drive entrance to Gratwicke is behind the engines.

Hammond's Farm, which is situated further up East Street is a typical local farmhouse, and dates from the seventeenth century. It has a Horsham stone roof and it is timber-framed under its brick façade. This and many other farmhouses in the parish are now family homes and no longer connected to working farms.

The ruins of Hammond's Mill in 1929. Hammond's Tower Windmill was built in 1825 and is situated near Hammond's Farm. The top of the windmill was blown off in a gale of 1906. The disaster was witnessed by Hugh Wadey, who was a local antiquarian.

Two

Around the Station
Area and Industries

Station Road did not exist before the coming of the railway. James King, the brewer, and Henry Puttock, who lived at Clevelands both gave strips of their land so that the width of Station Road could be improved. From Victorian to Edwardian times a number of substantial houses were built in both Upper and Lower Station Road. Mrs Maria Ireland, 1837-1918, said in reminiscences that there were no houses between the Vicarage and Kingsfold, Marringdean Road, except Broomfields, now Pennybrooks, and Great Daux, and no through road from Alicks Hill to Natts Lane. The railway made a great difference to the then rural region of the parish. Early industry moved to the area and has stayed there ever since. The first industry was the manufacture of wooden hoops for barrels, which were used for diverse purposes, but especially in the fish trade. When metal hoops for barrels became widespread the industry declined, although a few people were employed in the trade as late as 1950.

The Victorian Broomfield Lodge *c*. 1900. The name of the house has been changed to Knights and it now has a more elaborate façade. In turn James King, the Ireland family, William Henry Puttock, and Ray Stiles lived there.

Clevelands *c*. 1920. Another imposing Victorian residence of the Puttock family, which was pulled down when the second part of Cleve Way was built.

Station Road *c.* 1913, showing W T Voice's shop and probably one of his carriages. Station Road does not appear very busy.

The Malthouse in Station Road, in 1907. This malthouse was burnt down in 1883 and subsequently rebuilt with a house attached. In the last century James King owned the malthouse and the one situated in the High Street. The two ladies look very smartly dressed.

The malthouse was converted into The Whirlwind Carpet Sweeper Factory in early 1920s. The factory was later enlarged and a fashionable façade was added, although parts of the premises in the foreground were used as living accommodation.

The first annual "Whirlwind" outing to Brighton, 5 September, 1923. Ray Stiles, the American owner, standing second from the left, organised the factory efficiently and was a good employer. The work force also had its own sports teams, which competed against other sports sides in the neighbourhood. The management, standing in front of the coach, are all smoking.

Station Road in the 1950s. During the Second World War the factory was requistioned for war work. After 1945 Ray Stiles sold the plant and various firms used the premises; eventually the works were demolished and Weald Court flats were built on the site.

From *The Billingshurst News*. The "Cleaner Sweeper" was demonstated at the Wembley Exhibition of 1924. King George V purchased one for use in Buckingham Palace. The vacuum was created by a paddle wheel which was driven mechanically from the wheels, the only drawback was that the Whirlwind was not over effective.

William Thomas Voice outside his shop in Station Road *c.* 1935. Mr Voice senior always wore a bowler hat and white apron when serving in the shop. His three sons, William, Arthur "Bumper", and "Jack her up" Percy, all assisted him in the business, which the Voice family owned for more than fifty years. Many older residents have fond memories of the higgledy-piggledy shop.

Postal and Telegraphic Address :—" VOICE, GROCER, BILLINGSHURST."

W. T. VOICE,

Grocer and Fly Proprietor,

POST OFFICE, STATION ROAD, BILLINGSHURST.

Agent for the famous warranted brand " BOOTS & SHOES," best value can be obtained, try them.

HORSES & CARRIAGES, SINGLE OR PAIR, ON HIRE.

Rubber-Tyred Landau and Pair Horse Brake.

Sole Posting Agent for L. B. & S. C. Railway.

I REALLY feel I must rejoice
  I'm *leading* as the People's "*Voice*,"
And 'tis but right, for—as you know—
  Any event or local "Show,"
Which may *especial* notice court,
  Of it we make a "press" Report!

From Mrs Buskin's *Coronation Advertising Souvenir*, 1911.

Station Road in Edwardian times. The horse-drawn vehicle in the right foreground also belonged to W T Voice. His carriages waited at the station to pick up passengers alighting from the train; later he owned a model T Ford, which had to be jacked up to start. After Mr Voice senior died in 1949, his broughams, landaus, victorias and two horse-drawn hearses, making sixteen vehicles in all were sold to dealers in Edenbridge, Kent for only £20.

The Railway Hotel, now the Railway Inn. An added brick façade makes the building look very different today. The early level crossing gates and part of a station sign can also be seen.

The level crossing and signal box in the 1930s. The signal box is one of the earliest still in use in the region. F W Watt's Corn Merchants premises are in the background. F W Watt purchased the business in 1926, before that Walter Joyes owned it.

Billingshurst Station before the line was electrified by Southern Railway on 3 July 1938. The station was opened for passengers and freight as part of the London Brighton and South Coast Railway on 10 October 1859.

The Hoop Sheds, c. 1900, showing bundles of coppiced wood. Henry Puttock, who owned the hoop sheds, bought in bundles of trimmed wood from the locality. The firm moved to the station area, so the hoops could be transported directly from there. Before the railway was built the hoops were conveyed along the Wey and Arun Canal, from Newbridge.

William Botting, hoopbender. The sticks were sliced down the middle, then split and soaked in water to make them flexible. They were then taken to one of the ten hoop benches where they were made into hoops. Today nothing remains of the hoop sheds, although the cottage where William Botting lived still survives and is used for industrial purposes.

KILL IT!
WITH
KEATING'S

KEATING'S POWDER FLASK

1/-

No waste. Easier to use. Enables nooks and crannies to be reached without trouble. Costs 1/-. Can be refilled.

Even the cleanest home can be invaded by these detestable pests. Be prepared — have Keating's at hand. As a preventive, sprinkle a little Keating's Powder in nooks and crannies likely to harbour beetles and other troublesome insects.

From *The Billingshurst News*, 1930. Keating's Insect Powder was made in London from 1788, the firm moved to Daux Road in 1927. The process of making the powder was partly mechanised and very similar to milling. The Wylde family, who now own the factory, have been involved with the firm since the 1900s.

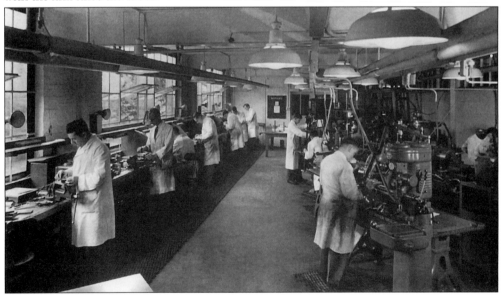

Thomas Keating, Ltd., during the Second World War. The firm was engaged in war work from 1940 and switched to making high quality precision tools. Later as the demand for insect powder declined this part of the business took over, which was quite a a jump from flea powder.

The staff of Keating's in 1970. There are some familiar faces here. The seated second row, left to right: Mrs Bradder, Win Penfold, -?-, Ron Boniface, Mr Buddle, Archie White, Eric Redford, Roy Bradder, John Wylde, Ronald Wylde, John Trot, Mark Albery. Other Billingshurst people include, Harold Chalk, Eric Baker, Mr Cherriman, Roger Pattison, Roger Zarins and Tim Etheridge.

An aerial view of the station, on a wet day, in 1939. This photograph was taken for Keating's before the factory was camouflaged at the beginning of the Second World War. Keating's premises are those with the light flat roof beyond the station. The extensive Whirlwind Factory site and F W Watt's buildings can also be seen in Station Road.

Great Daux, from a painting by H C Fox c. 1920. The house is now surrounded by industrial development, but for centuries it was the only farmhouse in the near vicinity. From the middle of the eighteenth century William Evershed, who was one of the founders of the Unitarian Chapel, lived at Great Daux, and the property stayed in Evershed hands for generations.

Dr Arthur Evershed, who was born at Great Daux in 1836. Arthur Evershed was first a professional artist, before becoming a doctor. Etchings of his are in several London Museums, and some of his early drawings of the village are rare pictorial records of Billingshurst before photography.

Lower Station Road, looking towards the station, *c.* 1913. Only a few changes have taken place in this part of Lower Station Road.

The corner of Lower Station Road, when there were fewer houses than today. On the right, Marycot is the first house in the middle distance. The building beyond that was a hall, now demolished, which was used by several different religious denominations at various times. (See under Churches).

Inside The Gas Works *c*. 1950. The North Sussex Gas and Water Company built The Gas Works about 1907. Eventually the works were taken over by British Gas and the buildings were demolished when North Sea Gas was installed in the locality.

Let your Fire
Go Out
When You Go Out.

FIT A

GAS FIRE.

For Terms and Particulars apply—
THE GAS WORKS,
Billingshurst.

A

GAS GEYSER

WILL SOON PUT

YOU

IN HOT WATER.

KEEP COOL!

USE A GAS
IRON.

DEMONSTRATED FREE

For Terms and Particulars apply
THE GAS WORKS,
Billingshurst.

Three advertisements from *The Billingshurst News*, 1931.

Herbert Topper stoking the furnaces at The Gas Works, c. 1950.

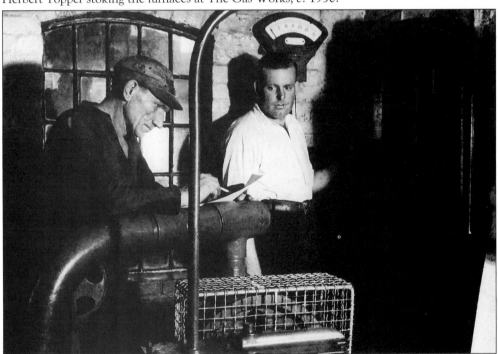

Herbert Topper and Vic Marchant inside The Gas Works. Gas lighting was introduced into the village in 1911. A "lights out" order was enforced during the First World War and it was not until 1923 that the lighting was reinstated. During the Second World War the lamps were kept at The Gas Works for safe-keeping. The Parish Council decided, in 1947, that the gas lighting was "A disgrace to the village", but it was not until 1956 that electric lights were finally installed.

Three

Heading for
the Hamlets

Besides the main village settlement and the station area there are several hamlets and other areas of habitation in the parish, such as Parbrook and Newbridge, as well as scattered farms and several large houses. Some of the farm settlements were probably started when downland manors claimed land in the parish for pig pasture: maybe as early as Saxon times tracts of the oak forest of the Weald were cleared and colonisation began. The two main hamlets are Adversane and Five Oaks, both of which are situated on Stane Street. Both hamlets were centres of small communities, with their own public house, small hall and shop. Five Oaks is situated at the north end of the parish. Five Oaks can be seen on Budgen's map of Sussex as early as 1724. Adversane is situated the south end of the parish. The old name for Adversane was Hadfoldsherne. A fine complex of timber-framed buildings can still be found there. Adversane held a relatively large annual fair where horses, cattle, pigs and corn were sold. Pork was always roasted and served in a large booth on the green. After 12 September, the date of the fair, pork was considered to be "In season locally". Newbridge belies its name, because it is an area of ancient settlement, the lost chapel of St Helen was situated somewhere nearby. Most of Newbridge was in Pulbourough parish until 1933.

Parbrook *c.* 1910. Part of the wall on the left is still standing. Parbrook is situated south of the village where the Parbrook, which is a tributary of the Arun, crosses Stane Street. The stream is now culverted at this point.

The restaurant and antiques business, which stand at the corner of Natts Lane at Parbrook, formerly a farmhouse and its barn, called Great Grooms, and later named Groomland Farm. Besides the timber-framed farmhouses still surviving in the parish there are also a number of early barns. In recent years some have been converted into houses.

Fossbrooks, the former home of the Wadey family, which is hardly changed today. Ephraim Wadey had his business premises adjoining the house. A young member of the family stands at the gate.

Ephraim Wadey who founded the Wadey's building firm in 1884. He died in 1915 and the business was carried on by his son Charles. In turn his two sons Raymond and Harold joined the firm and Charles Wadey & Sons was formed in 1934. Harold's son and Ephraim's great-grandson Alan joined the company in 1974.

A peaceful Edwardian view of Parbrook. A small child poses with a hoop and a horse grazes on the verge of what is now the busy A29.

The same view had changed little by the 1950s, but today the white house has been replaced with a more modern building housing Wadey's offices and Hurstlands estate has been built near the corner.

Adversane, showing Griggs and the row of cottages 1-7 Stane Street which were once yet another malthouse. Griggs, Old House and Southlands are all medieval houses; The Blacksmith's Arms is also timber-framed but not quite as old.

Old House c. 1960, which is an antiques business and restaurant. One room downstairs is reputed to be haunted by the ghost of an old man who sits with a broom in the inglenook fireplace. It is said that his presence can also be felt upstairs.

The Blacksmith's Arms and the old forge buildings to the left, the latter have been taken down. There was a resident blacksmith at Adversane for hundreds of years hence the name of the inn.

The interior of the Blacksmith's Arms which looks very dated by modern standards.

Gaius Carley, in his forge, *c*. 1960. Gaius was born in 1888 and had varied experience as a farrier in different parts of Sussex. He settled in Adversane in 1921 and earned sixteen shillings for his first week's wage. He wrote a book entitled *The Memoirs of Gaius Carley, a Sussex Blacksmith*, which gives interesting details about life in Adversane.

Outside the Limeburners, Newbridge in 1930, when it was a beerhouse. At this time only half the building was used as the Limeburners. The landlady, nicknamed "Mrs Whitestockings", stands behind the Billingshurst Angling Society Trophy with leading anglers. They fished in the nearby Arun and had their headquarters at the Limeburners. (See also page 122).

The river Arun at Newbridge, which is one of England's fastest flowing rivers. Man-made improvements to the course of the river allowed the Arun Navigation to become a transport system as far as Newbridge, from the late eighteenth century, before the canal was built.

Newbridge warehouse, which has now been restored. The warehouse, built in 1839, was part of a wharf, which served the Wey and Arun Junction Canal, which linked the Wey Navigation at Shalford with the Arun Canal at Newbridge. The canal, opened in 1816, was part of an inland waterway from the Thames to Littlehampton.

Rowner Lock in 1908. Owing to the coming of the railway the use of the canal quickly declined and the last barge passed through the lock in 1871. The lock was restored in 1982 by The Wey and Arun Canal Trust.

Rowner Mill from a dry point, which is similar to an etching, by Arthur Evershed, 1873.

The Water Wheel, c. 1908. The mill fell into disuse during the First World War and was demolished in 1968.

Rowner Watermill consisted of two separate mills with a connecting gallery beneath which was a public footpath. The older mill dated from around 1700, but a mill at Rowner was mentioned in documents dated 1539 and 1636. Rowner used to be in Pulborough, until the parish boundary took the course of the river.

Part of Okehurst Manor c. 1949. Okehurst, which is situated west of the village was a subsidary manor of Bassett's Fee, the main home manor of the parish. The white door frame has the date 1606 on it and the initials EG and HG, referring to the Goring family who held the manor at that time. Once again parts of the building are timber-framed under a brick façade.

The Five Oaks Inn, before 1909. Now the public house has a different façade, and the woman and girl stand where the driveway to Ingfield Manor is today. The pub was built *c*. 1850 and the Touse family were landlords for many years.

Ingfield Manor School in the harsh winter of 1963. The Fielding family of Okehurst Manor had Ingfield Manor built in 1909; they first called it Five Oaks Hall. In 1962 the family sold Ingfield to the Spastics Society, recently re-named Scope, and it has been a school for children with cerebral palsy ever since.

Five Oaks Farm, which is still a working farmhouse and the home of the Morris family. Although most of the house dates from Victorian times, parts of it are much older.

Robert Morris of Five Oaks Farm, who was the first chairman of the Parish Council, which was formed in 1895. He was also a benefactor to the people of Five Oaks, giving them the Iron Mission Hut in 1891, which was dismantled in 1989. (See also pages 100 and 125).

Ralph Wadey and Mr Port, c. 1960. The building business of James Wadey had its premises at Five Oaks, until the 1960s. It was another old established firm run by a Wadey family. However the owners of this business were not closely related to the other building company of Charles Wadey & Sons.

A Row of cottages on the A29, which look somewhat different today, because hanging tiles have been added to the façades.

Summers Place, in Edwardian times. The site is of ancient origin, but the present house was built in 1880 for Robert Goff; the architect was John Norton. The house was covered in ivy, like many other dwellings both large and small, at that time.

The hunt in front of Summers Place, which was sent as a Christmas card in December 1907.

Inside the entrance hall of Summers Place, which was bought by the Sisters of the Immaculate Heart of Mary in 1945 and became a girls' Convent School.

The Yew Walk, Summers Place, when it was the Convent of the Immaculate Heart of Mary. The school was closed in 1984 and the premises bought by Sotheby's Auctioneers and the buildings were converted to offices and auction rooms. The grounds make a very good background for the firm's sales of garden statuary.

Four
Churches and Chapels

There are four churches in the village, but the two non-conformist churches are sometimes still referred to as chapels. The Parish Church of St Mary is mainly perpendicular in style, but the earliest parts date from the twelfth century. The first recorded vicar was Thomas de Selhurst in 1274. The church has been added to and extended through the centuries and has many interesting features. It was extensively restored in 1866 when stone from Codmore Hill and Horsham was used. Nathaniel Hilton, the much loved parson who died in 1655, supported the Puritan cause. Later in the century Billingshurst Quakers began to attend the Friends Meeting House, which is in Thakeham parish, with William Penn. Several Billingshurst inhabitants went to America with Penn, the founder of Pennsylvania. The General Baptist Meeting House, now the Unitarian Church was established in 1754. The vestry was added in 1825 to contain the open baptistery; the last baptism took place in 1872. Until recent years the church had no water supply, therefore the baptistery had to be filled with water from the public well on the opposite side of the main road.

The Parish Church from Holywell Lane, c. 1938. The pond, which is to the right of the girls, disappeared about twenty-five years ago, like many others in the parish. In the distance the spire is being repaired in the time honoured hazardous way with the mender suspended in a basket. In 1766 two men fell to their deaths while re-shingling the spire when their tackle gave way.

From the sketchbook of Thomas Evershed, 1843. This is the earliest illustration in the book. Thomas emigrated to America but returned to England for a visit, during which time he made many sketches of the Sussex countryside. The low school building, behind the lady chapel, was removed in the 1866 restoration as well as the dormer windows in the nave.

A view of St Mary's Parish Church, c. 1950, before the churchyard was full and before Carpenter's Estate was built. The church stands on a commanding site overlooking the village. The heavy broach spire is a local landmark. The tower and the lady chapel, the outline of which can be clearly seen, date from the late twelfth century and are some of the earliest parts of the church.

A cedar tree in the churchyard blown down in a gale, in 1978, taken by Dr Bousfield. Mrs Ireland, 1837-1918, who was born in the old Billingshurst vicarage said in her reminiscences that John Allman planted the tree in 1844, in memory of his son John, because his favourite tree was a cedar.

The interior of St Mary's *c.* 1894. The church then had oil lighting and an earlier pulpit. This photograph was later used as a postcard.

The all male church choir *c.* 1921. Mrs Hingeston, the organist, is seated in the centre, behind her is the vicar, The Revd R O Johns. E Hingeston and John Argent, who were both churchwardens for many years, are on the extreme left and right of the back row. One of the choir boys is Alfred Lines, my husband's father.

The female side of the choir *c.* 1954. In the back row, left to right are Jane Langton the vicar's daughter, Anne Lusted, Jean Napper, Elizabeth Wolfe, Penny Hobson and June Day. Members of both Anne's and Jean's family appear in other photographs in the book.

The first Congregational Chapel and Meadow House, *c.* 1880. John Croucher purchased the octagonal wooden building in 1815, probably from Horsham where it had formerly been an Officer's Mess, during the the Napoleonic Wars. Meadow House is no longer aptly named as it stands behind Jengers Mead and is surrounded by modern development.

The Congregational Church, *c.* 1906. The present church was built in 1868, and it became the Trinity United Reformed Church in 1972. In 1885 a schoolroom was erected adjacent to the church, which is now used as a hall and in 1889 the manse, on the extreme left, was built partly with the proceeds from the sale of the old Jengers Chapel.

The Unitarian or Free Christian Church *c*. 1906. Formerly the General Baptist Meeting House founded in 1754 by William Evershed of Great Daux and William Turner of Newbridge, who purchased the site for three guineas. It is one of the oldest non-conformist churches in the district and in the churchyard can be found the graves of the "chapel" families, Turners, Carters and over 120 Eversheds.

The annual Anniversary Service at the Unitarian Church, 16 July 1973. Direct descendants of the founders still attend the "chapel", and in this congregation are many members of the Evershed and Carter families. Second from the left is J Dendy Evershed, who has traced and organised gatherings of the Evershed family from all over the world.

The Unitarian Church and it surroundings in 1970 (RCHME Crown Copyright). A housing estate has been built at the back of the "Chapel", so it has lost the rural background that it had for over two centuries.

Lower Station Road, c. 1907. The Gospel Hall seen in the middle of the postcard was built in 1888 and used by the Salvation Army and later by the Plymouth Brethren. The hall became the Roman Catholic Church in 1925 and a resident priest was appointed in 1933.

The Wedding of Eileen Maybee and Stam Romaniuck outside the Catholic Church, 1955. Emily Bristow is the eldest bridesmaid, the two little girl bridesmaids are Ann George and Jackie Aldridge. The photograph includes members of the Maybee, Romaniuck and Lines families.

The new St Gabriel's Roman Catholic Church. Mr and Mrs Maille, who lived in Marringdean Road, presented the parish with a plot of land in East Street in memory of their daughter and St Gabriel's Church was built there in 1961-2. The consecration of the new church did not take place until 1982, when all financial liabilities regarding its building were finally settled.

The Blue Idol, c.1907 There are several theories about how the Meeting House came by its rather pagan name. One is that the house was painted blue and it was for many years unused or idle, hence blue idol.

The Meeting Room of the Blue Idol c. 1920. The Society of Friends purchased the timber-framed building, formerly called Little Slatter, in 1691. Alterations were made to the south end of the house to make the meeting room.

Five

Schools and Schoolteachers

There is evidence of schools in Billingshurst from as far back as the sixteenth century. In the eighteenth century even pauper children in the workhouse were given some education. By the mid-nineteenth century there were several private schools: Mr Boorer kept an Academy and Miss Potter had a Boarding School for girls. At the east end of the parish church was a Chartered School for boys, which was described as ugly and which was pulled down in 1866. Both non-conformist churches provided some education, probably before the school run on national lines was established. This school was opened in 1861 and Henry Wright was the first headmaster; his wife, son and daughthers assisted him at the school. When he retired in 1906, his son Ernest, known as "Buzzy" Wright, succeeded him. Their combined period of service as headmasters was 68 years. The school building, in School Lane, East Street was the gift of Henry Carnsew of Summers Place in 1865. The new infants' building on the upper playground was added in 1912 and various huts were built. The original building was closed in 1973, although part of the site was used by the Junior School until 1991.

The Haven School, probably in the early 1900s. On the whole this school served a poorer, more rural community than the Billingshurst School. The children from Five Oaks attended The Haven School, which was in Slinfold parish, because it was nearer. The Haven School closed in 1948 and no trace of it remains. This photograph was rescued from a jumble sale about twelve years ago.

Pupils from Billingshurst School *c*. 1900. In the front row Emily Burrage holds the placard, the three Linfield sisters Kate, May and Nellie are in the same row. One little girl behind them is having a good yawn.

The old school, East Street, from the Infants' playground in the 1940s. In recent years this part of the school had fallen into disrepair, but fortunately both the main school buildings have now been converted into houses.

Empire Day, East Street, *c*. 1932. May 26 used to be a big day in the school calendar.

The first school canteen, 1931. Billingshurst was the first school in West Sussex to provide school meals. They were initiated by Mr Jeavons, the headmaster, who can be seen on the left. Edith and Ellen Beck of Duncans donated £50 to get the scheme started.

The Bowling Alley in the snow. Tom Topper said "At the bottom of the hill below the school was common ground called The Bowling Alley, we used to slide down on tin trays." Today the area is much more covered with vegetation and scrub, but in former times pupils were allowed to play in The Bowling Alley, which is still a favourite spot for tobogganing.

Dr Moreton with a Folk Dance Team, 1951. Back row, left to right: Eileen Napper, Nellie Russell, Joyce Denman, Margaret Brooker, Wendy Patrick and Frank Moreton. Second row: Doreen Hamilton, Pam Wicks, Heather Birchmore, Joan Laker, Sheila Riley, Doreen Hudson, Eileen Buddle. Front row: Sheila Radbourne, June Budgen, Myrtle Wells, Brenda Wells, Margaret Ledbetter, Iris Adams.

A victorious school football team, 1931/2. The team, left to right: Jack Matthews, Charlie Haddleton, Michael Kellehar, Fred Andrews, Eric Crisp, Tom Taylor. Front row: "Nutty" Elliott, Bert Quick, Geoff Voice, Harold Redman and Reg Denman

The staff of Billingshurst School *c*. 1949 Back row: Dr Moreton headmaster 1937-51, Mr Murphy, Front row: Miss Webb, who taught at the school 1917-50, Mrs Rankin and Miss Bristow. Frank Moreton had progressive ideas for his time; he held a School Council, which consisted of eleven pupils with Dr Moreton as chairman.

Weald Secondary School Staff, soon after the school opened in Station Road, in 1956. Left to right, back row: Miss Smith, Mr Ewins, Mr Elliott, Mr Flaxman, Mr Hall*, Mr Stevens, Mr Bentley, Mr Daniels, Mr Prior, Mr Dugdale*. Front row: Miss Lythgoe, Mrs Matthews*, Mrs Liley, Mr Gee the first headmaster, Mr Stone, Mrs Fosberry, Miss Halls and Mrs Davis. *Also taught at the old Billingshurst School. The senior part of Billingshurst School moved to the Weald School when it opened. The Weald officially became a Comprehensive School in 1969, and is now a Community School. Over 1,500 pupils from the area are educated there.

Six

Farming, Farm Machinery and Felling

Billingshurst has always been a farming community. In the fourteenth century the parish was poor in comparison with other surrounding communities, but by the seventeenth century, some yeoman farmers were prosperous, despite having to contend with the heavy clay soil. During Victorian times many changes took place in farming. The repeal of the Corn Laws in 1846 allowed the market to be swamped with imported grain. In the same decade the introduction of mechanisation caused unrest in rural areas. There was no recorded violence in Billingshurst, but times were harsh for the poor, and there was always the threat of the Workhouse if the lower classes fell on hard times. Some inhabitants went to seek a better life in Upper Canada by participating in an assisted emigration scheme. The fortunes of farming continued to fluctuate and later in the nineteenth century the agricultural depression continued owing mainly to cheap imports of meat and butter as well as the corn. In a parish of over 6,000 acres in the 1890s (7,975 acres in 1974), the main crops grown were wheat, oats, barley and roots. There were 1,000 acres of woodland: timber has always been important to the local economy. In addition there was some cattle, sheep and pig rearing, and dairy farming. There were about seven main landowners, besides more modest farmers, and still approximately 150 agricultural labourers. During the two World Wars there was a blockade on imported grain therefore much more home-grown corn was produced, especially during the Second World War. In the 1940s agriculture became more profitable, because of the vastly improved farming methods.

The Sherlock family and helpers after harvesting at Renvyle Farm, Okehurst Road, 1942. The corn rick has yet to be finished with a traditional thatched top. Jim Sherlock is seated in the front with his son David and daughter Sally. Standing second from the right is Iris Woods who was a land-girl at the farm for seven years. The Sherlocks are still one of the main farming families of Billingshurst. Over the years members of the family have been both parish and district councillors.

Lugg's steam traction engine and thresher, *c.* 1942, on the site of the Weald School. The grain from the thresher is being put into sacks by James Lugg. In his youth he was an apprentice at Carter Brothers: later he started his own business. On the extreme right is his son Gordon, who carried on the firm. Often the traction engine also operated an elevator to restack the threshed straw. The drum under the machine was used for steam ploughing. The outfit would have travelled from farm to farm to thresh corn.

A SUSSEX HARVEST FIELD: CUTTING OATS AT BILLINGSHURST

A Sussex Harvest field: cutting oats at Billingshurst, July 1939, from *The Times*. In recent years the cultivation of oats has declined. A self-binder can be seen in the background. All the machines illustrated were superseded by the combined harvester.

Haymaking at Clevelands during the Second World War.

"A Shady Nook" Billingshurst, *c*. 1940.

FIVE OAKS DAIRY,

BILLINGSHURST.

Telephone 66.

NOW DELIVERS GRADED

Milk in Billingshurst Area

TUBERCULIN TESTED (Certified) for
Nursery Use, thoroughly guaranteed
ACCREDITED MILK

Delivered within 1 mile Billingshurst Post Office.
Longer Distances extra.

KEEPING QUALITIES GUARANTEED 24 HOURS
AFTER DELIVERY, GIVEN FAIR TREATMENT.
OTHER SPECIALITIES :

RICH CREAM.   BUTTER.
NEW LAID EGGS.

PURE CREAM ICES

Made from Tuberculin-Tested Milk.
Dances, Garden Fetes, etc., supplied

From *The Billingshurst News*, 1930s. The Morris family owned the first milk floats in the area and operated the dairy from 1930 until 1970. Another milk-producing farm was Southlands at Adversane, run by the Voice family.

Baden Laker with Bill and Eddie Watt at Horsham Agricultural Show, *c.* 1953. F W Watt ran a successful corn merchants business from 1926, at Hereford House, Station Road. A third generation of the Watt family were still running the shop until it closed in 1992, much to the regret of many customers.

Sidney Carter *c.* 1935 at Loxwood Fair and Show. Sidney, James, Frank and Evershed Carter founded a firm of agricultural and general engineers, just outside the parish at Newpound, near the end of the nineteenth century. Carter Brothers work included mending farm machinery, and making wagon and cart wheels and manufacturing the well-known Unique Elevator. The Carters also developed the Reliance oil spring injection engine, as a small power unit for use on farms. Some zre still in operation.

Carter Brothers display at Horsham Argricultural Show, 1905, showing a Unique Elevator. This was used for lifting and stacking hay and straw, and was operated by the horse and post method of motive power and later by the steam engine and the oil engine.

One day's shipment of Unique Elevators at Billingshurst Station, 1929. Many older residents still remember the line of elevators waiting to be transported from the station.

The Lord Mayor's Show, London 1947, showing Land Girls working a Unique Elevator, the float was to promote National Savings.

A large tree felled by Carter Brothers, *c.* 1905, with interesting details of the wood-yard and saw-bench.

An oak tree felled by Ambrose Truelove and his gang of woodsmen, at Lordings. Every part of the tree was used, including the bark, in pieces in the foreground, for tanning.

Tanners Cottages, off the B 2133. Ambrose Truelove lived in one of the cottages for a while when he was first married. In other parts of the book are photographs of some of the parishes attractive farmhouses, but this building has been divided into several dwellings, and then had the typical appearance of Edwardian farm workers' cottages.

A rare rural scene *c.* 1906, taken from near Mill Lane. No trace of the barn remains, but it had coppiced wood stored in it. In contrast to the large trees felled, hazel, chestnut, ash and beech were cut regularly every seven or eight years, and in this region used mainly in the hoop industry. On the skyline can be seen the ruins of Hammond's windmill.

The tree must have been struck by lightening, but the wood is being put to good use. This postcard was bought at an Antiques Fair, and it was sent in 1927 by one of the Carter family to another member of the Unitarian Church, Miss E Kensett. All the other Carter Brothers photographs have come directly from the family.

Frank Pattison, 1871-1952, with his gun; there has always been good rough shooting in the area. "Pat" lived at Pear Tree Farm for over fifty years. He was an accomplished illustrator who worked for the *Cycling* magazine for many years. The Frank Pattison Appreciation Society is devoted to promoting his drawings, and there is an example of his work on Page 16. "Pat" liked to be thought of as a farmer – that is why he is included here.

Seven

Social Events, Societies and Sport

In bygone times outings were big events in the village calendar, Sunday School outings to the sea and school treats were looked forward to for months. "Buzzy" Wright stated in the School Log Book for Friday July 27 1924 "School closed on account of of School Excursion to Wembley" and he wrote on 30 July "The children had a very enjoyable and instructive day. ... We left Billingshurst at 7.30 by motor charabanc, and after a pleasant ride we arrived at Wembley at 10 o'clock. ... The educational side of the visit was kept in view only a limited portion of the time being spent in the Amusement Fair." At home organisations and societies held annual events. The Billingshurst Dramatic Society has been thriving for over fifty years, but the Billingshusrt Band did not survive. The Flower Show, run by the Horticultural Society, is still going, but the Bonfire Society no longer exists. The village in common with the rest of the country celebrated royal occasions with enthusiasm, the Coronation of King George V and Queen Mary is especially well photographed and recorded. There are of course many other organisations and sports clubs in the village and what follows is a limited selection.

The Council School off to the Wembley Exhibition, July 1924. Melville and Nigel Voice can be seen on the right wearing flat caps. From the School Log Book "The party consisted of 68 children the staff (3) and 12 adults (parents or older brothers or sisters) making a total of 83."

The Darby and Joan Club with their helpers, c. 1957. The group includes Mrs Lusted on the extreme right of the middle row, next to her stands "Ike" Freeman, Mrs Freeman is in front and Mrs Brown beside her at the end of the row. First on the left back row is Mr Wakeling with Mrs Wakeling in front of him. Mr Williams the coach operator, is fourth from the right back row.

A mystery photograph, taken outside Ye Olde Six Bell, maybe as early as 1885. It is probably The United Tradesmen's Friendly Society Annual Club Day, which took place in June from 1832. The Laker family, who own the photograph think that Henry Laker, who was born in 1857, is one of the young men in the group.

The Billingshurst Amateur Dramatic Society drumming up support in the the High Street, 1963. Left to right John Farmer, Charles Leaman, John Humphreys, Jack Leaman and Robert Hall.

A Billingshurst Dramatic Society production, of *The Rivals* in 1942. The cast includes Mrs Patsy Sherlock on the far left with George Hook, Frank Moreton is third from right. The BDS was founded in 1941 and produce three plays a year of a high standard at the Women's Hall. There are records of previous amateur dramatic performances, going back to the last century.

Julia Kelly, John Farmer and John and Rene Humphreys in a 1966 Dramatic Society production of *The White Sheep of the Family*.

Billingshurst Band in Gingers Field. The band was formed in 1919 and in 1921 the Misses Beck of Duncans provided the band with a complete set of uniforms.

The Band, led by Archie Stanton, who was the last band-leader, in the 1940s. Besides playing at local functions the band entered and won band competitions.

BILLINGSHURST.
VEGETABLE, FRUIT, AND
FLOWER SHOW.

THE EXHIBITION
WILL BE HELD BY KIND PERMISSION OF
L. R. ERSKINE, Esq.,
PRESIDENT FOR THE YEAR,
AT
SUMMERS PLACE,
ON
WEDNESDAY, AUGUST 10, 1904.

The Grounds will be opened at 3 p.m., & closed at 8 p.m.
NONE of the Articles to be removed before 7.30.

THE HORSHAM TOWN BAND
WILL BE IN ATTENDANCE.

SPORTS TO COMMENCE AT 5 O'CLOCK.

Miss LUKIN has kindly consented to distribute the PRIZES at 6 o'clock.

Admission, 3 till 5, 1s. After 5, 3d. CHILDREN UNDER 12, 1d.

ALL ENTRIES TO BE SENT TO MR. LUXFORD, A WEEK BEFORE THE SHOW.

Printed by E. Wright, Billingshurst.

The first Flower Show was held at Summers Place in 1882. Until 1950 The Flower Show was always held on a Wednesday, Billingshurst's early closing day. The Horticultural Society, which runs the show, still flourishes and is one of Billingshurst's oldest organisations.

112

The last Flower Show to be held in a marquee, in the Recreation Ground, Lower Station Road, in 1969. Since 1970 the show has been held at the Weald School. Two judges, wearing the suits, are with Joe Kingston and John Sutton, two officials of the Horticultural Society.

Wally Wicks, who was a great gardener, after winning The Society's Cup for gaining the most points in the show in 1969. Major-General Renton, of Rowfold Grange, who was president of the Society, Alan Dugdale, hon. secretary and John Sutton.

Billingshurst Bonfire Society.

GRAND FANCY DRESS

TORCHLIGHT PROCESSION,

WEDNESDAY, NOVEMBER 5th, 1930.

The Proceeds will be given to the Horsham Hospital, District Nursing Association, and the Billingshurst Hospital Letters (Ambulance) Fund.

PRIZES FOR FANCY DRESS COMPETITIONS.

CLASS.   SECTION ONE

A. Lady's Character Costume   1st, 2nd & 3rd Prizes
B. Gent's   do.   do.   ,,   ,,   ,,
C. Juvenile's do.   do.   ,,   ,,   ,,

SECTION TWO.

D. Lady's Comic Costume   1st, 2nd & 3rd Prizes
E. Gent's   do.   do.   ,,   ,,   ,,
F. Juvenile's do.   do.   ,,   ,,   ,,

Also Three Prizes for the Most Original Costumes and Three Prizes for the Best Home-made Costumes (Lady's, Gent's & Juvenile in each Class).

ENTRANCE FEES: **Adults** (including membership) **2/-**
Juveniles under 17 (including Membership) **1/-**

RULES.

These Competitions are open to all Members, and will take place at the VILLAGE HALL, Billingshurst, on Wednesday, November 5th.

JUDGING at 6.30 p.m., sharp. There must be not less than six Competitors in each Class.

The Hall will be thrown open to the Public after the Judging.

All Costumes must be worn by the Competitors in the Procession.

No Competitor may take more than one Prize in the Classes, but may compete in the Most Original and the Home-made Costumes.

All Competitors must give in their Names to **Mr. W. J. Barnes** (opposite the Post Office) **by 8.0 p.m. on Tuesday, November 4th.**

Charles Tiller, Printer, Billingshurst, Sussex.

Bonfire night was a big event in the days of the Bonfire Society, which was founded around 1880. The Society ceased to function in the 1950s but was reformed again 1969-73.

114

Bonfire Night Fancy Dress, in 1954, right to left: Don Everson, "Nobby" Clark, Denny Adams.

Pat Hollybone, Nellie Maybee and Betty Burchell dressed for the Bonfire Night Fancy Dress, c. 1953.

The Women's Institute visit to Windsor from Kingston, 1937. Even though his wife went on the trip, Charles Tiller wrote in *The Billingshurst News*, "Once more we regret we can secure no coherent account of the day's happenings."

Freddie Wells collecting at Adversane for the Guy Fawkes Committee, in the early 1950s Freddie, who was a professional gardener, played cricket for Billingshurst in his younger days and was a founder member of the Angling Society. (See page 122).

Floral Parade, 1910, in the High Street. The Revd Stanley wrote in The Parish Magazine "A Queen of Roses, carrying a miniature maypole, surrounded by a bevy of boys and maidens wearing rustic dresses and singing sweetly as they went, was particularly worthy of comment. A Royal Red Cross hospital van brought up the rear, for effect picked up some mites who were over-fatigued by the journey."

Hillview Garage decorated for the Coronation of King George V1, 1937. The garage was then only on the east side of Stane Street.

Coronation Parade, 1911. The coronation of King George V was celebrated in grand style in the village. Mrs Buskin's Booklet and Supplementary Verses can be linked to photographs. There are at least seven different shots taken from the green. The boy in the light suit and hat was as interested in the photographer as the parade.

The Empire Cart, 1911. Mrs Buskin produced Supplementary Verses, after her booklet so "The youthful people in Billingshurst will thus have pleasure seeing their names in print." On the far right can be seen Miss Dorothy Balchin dressed as Britannia. Elizabeth Buskin said about her "Oh! stately form with Union Jack draped tastefully around, That 'Flag' which signals to the world it stands for British ground!"

Tossing up before a Fancy Dress Charity Stool-ball match at East Street School Fete, 1955. The teams include Marjorie Lugg, GeorgeWhite, Tom Walker, Hilda Matthews, Tom Topper, Oliver Hall and Mr Dutton.

Members of the Bowling Club and their families, c. 1935, outside the Club House off Station Road. The group includes on the extreme right Frederick Lusted, seated third from right is his wife, second from right Mrs Crisp and first on the right Mrs Williams, behind the bowls is Elizabeth Williams, and David Williams sits in front of his mother. Frank Williams is holding a trophy third from left back row, next to him is Mr Crisp, with a pipe in his mouth, (a tobacconist and hairdresser, his shop appears in several photographs). Geoffrey Duke sits on his mother's lap in the front row.

A victorious football team outside the King's Head in 1920. "Buggy" Wadey, the captain is in the middle of the front row. The Billingshurst Football Club celebrated its centenary in 1990.

Billingshurst football team, (WSCT copyright) 1963/64 was another triumphant season. Back row, left to right: Alex Harvey chairman, B Elliott, R Elliott, J Vardy P Hotson, D Clarke, G Poat, P Harrison, R Pattison, Front row: G New, J Chalaye, R Claydon, E Baker, K Landford, L Clarke captain, and L Denman secretary.

The cricket team, date unknown. The cricket field has been in Station Road since the early Victorian era. One of the team was Caleb Hughes, but it is not known whether Dr Hubert is in the photograph. He was a good batsman and was reputed on one occasion to have hit a ball on to the railway line and several times to have hit a six over the houses in Station Road!

The President's match, 1965. (WSCT copyright) The Billingshurst team stand behind Dr Hope-Gill the President and Roger Lusted. Left to right: David Patten, Peter Fautly, Gordon Albery, Brian Smith, John Farmer, Ken Pavey, Herbie Parsons, Alan Gosling, in front Eric Baker and hidden at the back John Hale.

Winning Anglers, 1930, outside the Limeburners. (See also page 72). The group includes back row, left to right: Charlie Isted, and Ambrose Truelove with the eye-patch. Front row, right to left: Ned Haylor and and Freddie Wells.

Members of the Angling Society in the 1950s. Left to right: Duncan Reynolds, Don Everson, Les Grinstead, in front Peter Kyte and Danny Cherriman. The same trophy was on display in the previous photograph.

Eight
The Two World Wars

During the First World War the Parish's casualty figures and home front war effort were faithfully recorded by the vicar in the Parish Magazine. The Revd R O Johns commentary is poignant because his own "very dear son" was one of the 55 young men of Billingshurst who died for their country during the conflict. The vicar wrote "The 50th name had been added to our Roll of Honour for the dead - Arthur Garton. The bell tolled at noon 50 strokes when the sad tidings came." During the Second World War many of the larger houses were requistioned. Officers stayed at Tedfold, Okehurst and Knights. Many Canadian troops were stationed in the area. Those at Wooddale Camp used to invite local children to parties, these are still fondly remembered today by some middle-aged people who were children in the 1940s. Many of the Canadian soldiers lost their lives during the Dieppe landing. On the home front the Civil Defence, Home Guard and Royal Observer Corps were all very active. For a short while in 1944 at nearby Coolham an Advanced Landing Ground was in operation. Fifteen airmen were killed flying from here in a few months. Eleven men of the parish died on Active Service during the Second World War.

YOUR KING AND COUNTRY THANK YOU
Christmas Greetings from your Friends at Billingshurst, 1917.

King George V thanks a soldier and a sailor, 1917. A well-designed patriotic mass produced card with Billingshurst stamped on it. Behind the sailor is a church lych-gate and behind the soldier rustic folk, all on the background of the Union Flag

A Cavalry detachment resting at Gratwicke Park, during its journey to the French battlefields, in the First World War.

The War Memorial was unveiled on 13 February 1921. From The Parish Magazine "The ceremony of the unveiling will be performed by the Billingshurst man who won the highest honour in the War; the names of the men commemorated will be read; then the Cross will be dedicated." Lieut. Gordon Mackie, MC performed the ceremony. He was a scout-master, both before and after the First World War.

On the left Robert William Morris of the Lancashire Fusiliers, Bill survived the war and later inherited Five Oaks Farm. On the right Second Lieutenant Francis Morris of The Queen's Regiment. Francis was killed in September 1916 in Mesopatamia. Their brother James, who was in the Royal Sussex Regiment, also survived, but a fourth brother Lieutenant John Child Morris of the Welsh Regiment died in August, 1915 at Gallipoli. In St Mary's Church there are beautiful wooden memorial doors dedicated to the two brothers who were killed.

The Fire Service and Auxillary Fire Service parading, near Chapel corner, South Street, in the 1940s. A large number of local people were involved with civil defences.

Trooper Percy Napper of the 4/R. Tanks, who was killed at Tobruk on 22 November 1941 aged thirty-one. His name is on both the Rudgwick and Billingshurst War Memorials. He left a widow and two small daughters; his sister Rhoda had the misfortune to be killed with her husband when a bomb fell on Orchard Road Horsham, in 1940.

The prisoner of war camp, Marringdean Road, 1945 (*The Soldier* Magazine copyright). Cpl K Lewis checks in a party of German prisoners returning from work in the fields. Italian prisoners were first detained in the camp, they were then followed by Germans. Some of the latter settled in the area after they were released. For many years the site was a riding stables and now it is a housing estate.

"We shall defend every Village, every Town and every City"...

THE PRIME MINISTER.

BILLINGHURST SOUTH STREET.

And so say all of us.

The last picture shows one of the most photographed views of the village superimposed on a massed produced postcard. On the back is printed "Published by permission of the Prime Minister."

Acknowledgements

There is abundant material on Billingshurst, but very little published about the parish, therefore I have made use of many different sources for the both the text and illustrations and would like to thank numerous people and organisations. Firstly the Billingshurst Local History Society for the use of their photographic collection and archives. I owe a debt of gratitude to the late Ricky Myers who gave the Society his photographs of the village and started the collection.

I must particularly express my appreciation to Gordon Simkin for his help in preparing the photographs. I am also especially grateful to Cyril Roffe for access to his extensive postcard collection and to Duncan Reynolds for tracking down and borrowing elusive photographs.

My warm thanks go to Lindsey Voice for the use of copies of *The Billingshusrt News*, family papers and photographs and for happy hours spent looking through them with her. I owe very many thanks to Mary Evershed for allowing her grandfather's artistic works to be published and for the pleasure of the time passed with her.

I am indebted to the West Sussex Record Office, The Billingshurst Women's Institute, the vicar, Canon D Pain and J Luckin headmistress of the County Junior School, for the use of their archives and photographs.

I am grateful to *The West Sussex County Times*, *The Soldier* Magazine, and The Royal Commission on Historical Monuments England. I thank also *The West Sussex Gazette*, *The Times* and Horsham Museum.

Many thanks are owed to the people who so generously gave their time recalling the past and who loaned postcards and entrusted me with unique family photographs and drawings. They are Mr B Baker, Mrs H Barton, Mrs L Baxter, Mr & Mrs R Boniface, Mrs E Cansell, Mr R Carter, Mr & Mrs C Clark, Mr & Mrs E Cripps, Mrs L Donaldson, Mr D Evans, Mr J D Evershed, Mr D Everson, Mr J Farmer, Mr K Geary, Mr D Hook, Mrs R Howard, Mrs I Humphreys, Miss R Kellehar, Mr M Laker, Mrs J Lewington, Mrs C Luckin, Mr G Lugg, Mr M Lugg, Mr I Lusted, Mr & Mrs R Lusted, Mr & Mrs S Marshall, Mr E Merrikin, Mr G Moore, Mr & Mrs J Morris, Mr R Norris, Mr A Quick, Mr C Rhodes, Mrs P Roberts, Mr & Mrs J Russell, Mr C Sawyer, Mrs P Sherlock, Mrs J Stanley, Mrs M Stenning, Mr P Tabb, Mrs A Topper, Mr T Topper, Miss C Voice, Mrs J Voice, Mr & Mrs H Wadey, Mr D Watt, Dr J Wylde and Mrs A Young. Thanks as well to Billingshurst Dramatic Society, The Frank Pattison Appreciation Society and The Wey and Arun Canal Trust.

For information about Billingshurst buildings I would like to thank Diana Chatwin, Robert Dames, Marjorie Hallam, John Hurd, Peter Lines and Paul Smith.

I am grateful to Martin Hayes, Principal Librarian Local Studies, West Sussex for his invaluable advice. Warm thanks are also due to Janet Austin, Rhonwyn Daniel and Linda Lines for their advice, encouragement and corrections of the text.

I have as far as possible checked the authenticity of the material and I am sorry for any omissions in the acknowlegements. I also apologise to anyone else whose copyright I may have inadvertently breached.